flourishing postpartum PLANNER

YOUR GUIDE TO THE FOURTH TRIMESTER.

created by: Tijana McAllister

All rights reserved. No Part of this publication may be reproduced, distributed, or transmitted in any form or by any means, including photocopying, recording or other electronic methods, without the prior written permission of the author, except in the case of brief quotations in a book review or non commercial uses.

COPYRIGHT @ 2024 TIJANA MCALLISTER
FIRST EDITION
ISBN PAPERBACK: 978-1-0688323-0-7

The author has made every attempt to provide information that is accurate and complete, but this planner is not intended as a substitute for professional medical advice.

Chapters

01. INTRODUCTION.....................7
What is Flourishing Postpartum and how did it start. Meet Tijana the twin mama and postpartum doula and her story of wanting to help mamas thrive.

02. WHAT IS POSTPARTUM........15
First we will go over what happens during postpartum and how you can prepare. Showing how a solid plan for yourself, your baby and family can help.

03. NUTRITION & MEALS...........27
How do you manage a new baby and meal planning plus feeding your body healthy meals. Here let's focus on meal plans, freezer meals and postpartum nutrition.

04. BECOMING A MAMA............43
The postpartum period can be a beautiful time. Knowing what to expect when it comes to your body, mood and healing will help you feel confident stepping into your new role mama!

05. SUPPORTING BABY...............65
Taking the time, before baby arrives, to understand what a newborn needs, how they sleep, what a breastfeeding schedule looks like and the support you may require.

06. FAMILY EDUCATION............85
During pregnancy is a great idea to prepare your family. Make sure everyone is on the same page when it comes to sleep, visitors, feeding and mental health.

Chapters

07. PARTNER PLAN..................99

Sitting down to create a plan with your partner is crucial for your postpartum support mama. Knowing what your nights will look like, where the baby will sleep, and how you can support one another.

08. YOUR SUPPORT TEAM.......111

In this section we will list all of the people who will help you after your baby arrives. Define their roles, tell them where you may need help and have a call list on hand.

09. YOU'VE GOT THIS!..............121

You've done it! Created a postpartum plan so you can feel prepared and supported during the fourth trimester. Let's review. Plus some wonderful bonuses.

10. POSTPARTUM DOULA.......133

A little note from Tijana on how being a postpartum doula has allowed her to support many mamas on their journey.

Chapter 01

INTRODUCTION TO FLOURISHING POSTPARTUM

MEET TIJANA A POSTPARTUM DOULA & TWIN MAMA

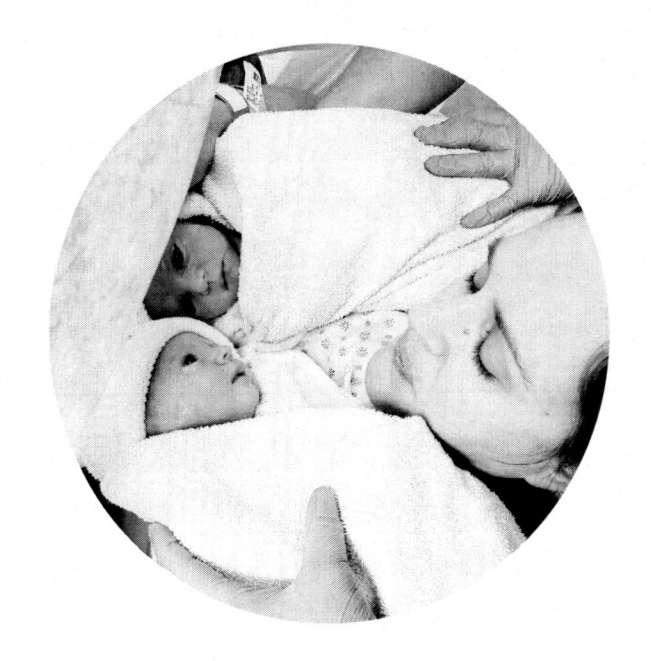

WELCOME MAMA!

Mama, my hope with this postpartum planner is it will help you feel confident stepping into motherhood. Any questions, concerns or doubts you may have will be answered or a plan created for them. I want to take the stress out of postpartum so you can simply focus on yourself, the new baby and your family. By making a plan before the baby arrives you will know where you need support, your partner/family will know how they can help and on hard days there will be a meal in the freezer.

Birth lasts hours, but postpartum is months (or now the data suggests years). Creating a plan that supports you, mama, will make all the difference in your postpartum journey.

Tijana

01 / MY STORY

I was unprepared so you won't be. Evie and Poppy arrived 5 weeks early and although I had all the cute baby clothes, adorable nursery and baby gear checked off. I'd forgot the most important piece, ME! Besides a few freezer meals, I hadn't created a postpartum plan for myself. Who was my support team, how was breastfeeding supposed to work and where was the time for me to recharge?

Combine all that with how I was feeling emotionally (coming down off twin pregnancy hormones is intense), physically (an emergency cesarean will do that) and mentally (I knew I needed help but didn't know how to ask), I definitely struggled. Then I decided I could help other mamas create a plan to FLOURISH postpartum.

> **"EVIE AND POPPY ARRIVED 5 WEEKS EARLY AND ALTHOUGH I HAD ALL THE CUTE BABY CLOTHES, ADORABLE NURSERY AND BABY GEAR CHECKED OFF. I'D FORGOT THE MOST IMPORTANT PIECE, ME!"**

Flourishing Postpartum was born to help new mamas. Did you know the postpartum period is the time after birth up to a year following? (Now it's said to be several years!) Most mamas think or are told after their 6 week check up they will be back to themselves. Until you actually arrive at the milestone and realize there might be more work to do.

When we use the word postpartum it doesn't mean depression or anxiety, although it can. Postpartum is simply the period of time after childbirth where a mother's body, including hormone levels and uterus size return to their non-pregnant state. More importantly where a mama recovers physically and emotionally from her pregnancy and birth and steps into a new season of motherhood.

WHAT'S IN A POSTPARTUM PLAN

Does the idea of creating a postpartum plan overwhelm you? Are you worried you won't know the answer. This is why we are here, to take the time and create a plan together before your baby arrives. If you're baby has already arrived and you need a plan, it's never too late.

In the Flourishing Postpartum Plan you will learn about postpartum and create a plan to support you during this time. By doing this you can take away the worry, overwhelm and anxiety that can sometimes come with postpartum. Replacing it with joy, confidence and support

If any questions come up, or your not sure who to include in your support circle, or you're feeling overwhelmed with planning. I am always here. Feel free to reach out any time. I'm available to make sure mamas are prepared for postpartum. hello@flourishingpostpartum.com

Tijana

MAMA CHECK IN

TAKE A MOMENT

Mama, how are you feeling about postpartum? Is it something you've thought about? Are you worried now you've only planned for the baby and not yourself? Does it feel like a lot of work to read this postpartum planner? Are you feeling overwhelmed at creating a postpartum plan? I think all of these feelings are valid. I promise you, this work will pay off when your baby arrives. You will set yourself up to be supported, confident about what to expect and prepared for yourself.

What feels overwhelming about postpartum?

_____
_____
_____
_____
_____
_____

What energy do you want in your postpartum experience?

_____
_____
_____
_____
_____
_____

POSTPARTUM VISION

LET'S START CREATING A PLAN

Mama, maybe you know how you want to feel in your postpartum period, but writing it down will help you get clear on what you want, who will be there, how you can be supported, what your expectations are and any feelings of overwhelm, fear or worry. With this information we will start to craft your personal postpartum plan as you work through the Flourishing Postpartum Planner.

How does your ideal postpartum look? Who's there?
What help do you need? Where will meals come from?

_____
_____
_____
_____
_____
_____
_____
_____
_____
_____
_____
_____
_____
_____

"POSTPARTUM IS A BEAUTIFUL SEASON WHERE WE GET TO SIT IN AWE OF OUR BABY AND BODIES. LEAN INTO THAT."

Tijana

Chapter 02

WHAT IS THE POSTPARTUM PERIOD?

LOOKING AT A POSTPARTUM DEFINITION, TIMELINE AND MYTHS

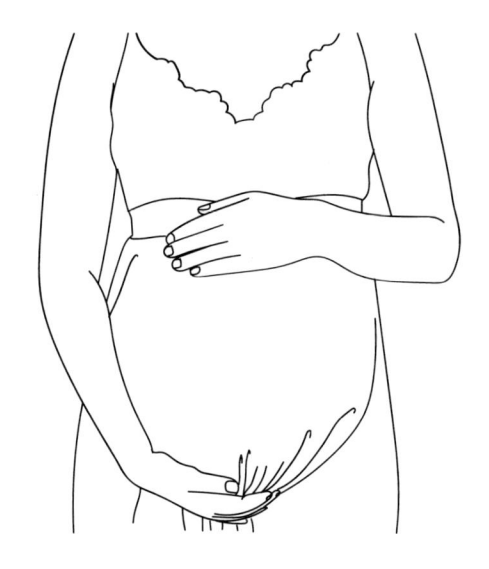

LET'S DISCOVER THE POSTPARTUM PERIOD

I'm sure you've heard a lot about postpartum through your pregnancy, some scary and others lighthearted. Does it all still feel a little unknown? To me it did. Let's define postpartum, address different postpartum myths and take a look at a postpartum timeline.

This chapter is great to review before the baby is born and also reference once they are here. Sometimes while healing from birth or moving through the fourth trimester, you may wonder if what is happening is normal? I've included a timeline of the postpartum period, not everyone will follow this exactly but it can give you an idea of what to expect.

Let's Discover Postpartum

02/ DEFINITION OF POSTPARTUM

During pregnancy a woman's body undergoes many changes to support the baby's development. After giving birth, the body will slowly start to return to it's pre-pregnancy state. This process is known as postpartum period or the fourth trimester. There are a few key changes happening during this time:

PHYSICAL RECOVERY: The uterus will start to return to its normal size, any tears from a vaginal birth or incisions from a cesarean will start to heal and the postpartum bleeding (lochia) will start to lessen.

HORMONAL CHANGES: Estrogen and Progesterone both decrease as soon as the baby and placenta are birthed. This hormonal shift can cause mood swings and emotional changes.

EMOTIONAL ADJUSTMENT: A range of emotions can be felt during the postpartum period, from joy over your new baby to feelings of overwhelm, exhaustion and sadness. In early postpartum this is called the Baby Blues.

INFANT CARE & BONDING: Learning to care for you new born, establishing breastfeeding and milk supply plus bonding with your baby. There's a lot to take in during the postpartum period.

02/ POSTPARTUM TIMELINE

Let's look at what happens for mama and baby after birth. This covers the postpartum period or fourth trimester from 24 hours to 6 months.

Hours 24
- Bonding with your baby
- Initiating breastfeeding
- Uterus starts to reduce in size
- Lochia discharge/ postpartum bleeding

Week 01
- Postpartum "baby blues"
- Estrogen & Progesterone drop
- Healing tears or cesarean incisions
- Establishing a breastfeeding rhythm

Week 02
- Lochia or bleeding continue
- Vaginal soreness or discomfort
- Cesarean scar may itch or feel numb
- Night sweats could start

02/ POSTPARTUM TIMELINE

Let's look at what happens for mama and baby after birth. This covers the postpartum period or fourth trimester from 24 hours to 6 months.

Week 04
- Postpartum bleeding may decrease
- Baby's feedings may be more established
- May still look pregnant as uterus shrinks
- Exhausted but feeling more like yourself

Week 06
- Postpartum check up around this time
- Easing into gentle exercise & movement
- Uterus back to pre-pregnancy size
- Bleeding stops, though can restart

Months 2-3
- May notice postpartum hair loss
- Hormones return to pre-baby levels
- Prolactin & oxytocin stay high if breastfeeding
- Possible milk supply issues

02/ POSTPARTUM TIMELINE

Let's look at what happens for mama and baby after birth. This covers the postpartum period or fourth trimester from 24 hours to 6 months.

Months 3-4
- Vaginal delivery wounds healing
- Found & established breastfeeding rhythm
- Notice postpartum hair regrowth
- Feeling more emotionally stable

↓

Months 4-6
- Hair should stop falling out
- Full bladder control should return
- Period may come back at this time
- Positive feelings and time for self care

LET'S LOOK AT POSTPARTUM MYTHS

There are several myths and misconceptions surrounding new mamas and the postpartum period. These myths can sometimes create unrealistic expectations or add unnecessary pressure on new mamas.

Challenging these myths and understanding the realities of the postpartum period can help new mamas navigate this transformative time with more confidence and self-compassion. Every new mama's experience is unique, and it's essential to prioritize well-being, seek support when needed, and celebrate the joys and challenges of motherhood.

Common Postpartum Myths

02/ POSTPARTUM MYTHS

EVERY MAMA INSTANTLY BONDS WITH HER BABY

REALITY: While many new mamas do feel an immediate bond with their baby, it's also normal for bonding to take time. The bond between a mama and her child can develop gradually over the early weeks and months.

BREASTFEEDING IS EASY & NATURAL FOR ALL MAMAS

REALITY: Breastfeeding can be challenging for some mamas and babies. It may require time, patience, and support to establish a successful breastfeeding relationship. Not all mamas are able to breastfeed exclusively. What matters most is that the baby is well-fed and thriving.

MAMAS SHOULD EASILY "BOUNCE BACK"

REALITY: The postpartum body goes through significant changes, and it's unrealistic to expect rapid body transformation. It takes time for the body to heal and recover after childbirth. Emphasizing self-acceptance and self-care during this time is crucial.

MAMAS SHOULD BE HAPPY ALL THE TIME

REALITY: The postpartum period is a time of intense emotions, and it's normal to experience a range of feelings, including joy, sadness, anxiety, and exhaustion. It's essential to recognize and address any emotional challenges with support and understanding.

NEW MAMAS SHOULD BE ABLE TO DO IT ALL

REALITY: It's okay to ask for help and support from family, friends, or professionals. Caring for a newborn can be overwhelming, and having a support system can make a significant difference in a new mama's well-being.

MAMAS SHOULD PRIORITIZE THE BABY

REALITY: Self-care is crucial for new mamas. Taking care of one's physical and emotional needs is essential for overall well-being and the ability to care for your baby.

POSTPARTUM DEPRESSION IS A SIGN OF WEAKNESS

REALITY: Postpartum depression is a common and treatable condition that affects many new mamas. It's not a sign of weakness but rather a combination of hormonal, emotional, and situational factors. Seeking help and treatment is essential for recovery.

NEW MAMAS SHOULD "KNOW" WHAT TO DO

REALITY: Caring for a newborn is a learning process. It's okay to seek guidance and support from healthcare providers, parenting resources, and experienced mamas. Getting to know your baby takes time.

DON'T BELIEVE EVERYTHING ONLINE

REALITY: Becoming a mama is a life-changing experience. Give yourself time to get to know your baby, discover your postpartum body, sit with your emotions and find your own rhythm.

MAMA CHECK IN

TAKE A MOMENT

Mama, please keep in mind this is a general timeline and definition of postpartum. Every mamas experience is different. Having a guideline is great to check in with yourself. Remember every postpartum period is unique. Now let's look at a few ways you can support yourself in the early days of the fourth trimester.

What are a few ways to support your unique postpartum journey?

Example: limit social media in the early days. Learning to trust your baby & intuition.

_____
_____
_____
_____
_____
_____

How will you remember to reference this in postpartum when you feel unsure?

_____
_____
_____
_____
_____
_____
_____

"BIRTH LASTS HOURS, POSTPARTUM IS MONTHS. LET'S START PLANNING FOR POSTPARTUM SO MAMA CAN FEEL SUPPORTED AND CONFIDENT"

Tijana

Chapter 03

POSTPARTUM NUTRITION & MEALS

HOW TO SUPPORT YOUR ENERGY, HEALING AND BABY.

WHY IS NUTRITION SO IMPORTANT IN POSTPARTUM

I thought the few freezer meals and snacks in our freezer would be good enough, I was wrong! There's much more to consider when it comes to postpartum nutrition. Have you considered a meal train? Do you know what foods are helpful for postpartum healing? Where will you keep a meal planner?

Do you know that nutrition can be vital for postpartum healing and energy. Not only that it can aid sleep, mood and support your body in caring for your baby and breastfeeding. Food is important but we are going to look specifically at the nutrients to support your postpartum body. Then we will create a plan to make sure you are prepared before the baby arrives.

Start Nourishing Your Body

03/ NOURISHING YOUR BODY

Nutrition and healthy eating are so important for your body, energy levels, sleep, healing and baby in postpartum. Although it can be easy to work your way through the snack cupboard, you probably won't feel your best. During the postpartum period your body needs a lot of support and that includes the right nutrition.

Things to consider:

01. Preparing food before the baby arrives

02. Eating a balanced diet to support your postpartum body

03. Creating a meal plan or two before you give birth

04. Ordering grocery delivery or a meal service

05. Always have snacks ready!

06. Have a friend create a meal train for the first few weeks postpartum

03/ POSTPARTUM NUTRITION

The nutrients needed during the initial postpartum period, especially while breastfeeding, are higher than while pregnant. This is not a time to worry about counting calories or losing weight or getting back into your skinny jeans. In early postpartum it's about supporting your body with nutrition to aid with healing, breastfeeding, mood and sleep.

PROTEIN-RICH FOODS: Protein helps in tissue repair and boosts postpartum energy levels.
- **Food Sources:** eggs, lean meat (chicken or turkey), fish, legumes, slow cooked meats, nuts and seeds

IRON-RICH FOODS: Blood loss during childbirth and breastfeeding can reduce iron stores. These foods help to increase iron levels.
- **Food Sources:** spinach, lentils, lean red meat, tofu and beans, fortified cereals, liver

HEALTHY FATS: These are important for hormone production, tissue repair and brain health.
- **Food Sources:** avocado, nuts (almonds and walnuts), seeds (chia and flaxseed), and olive oil

OMEGA-3 FATTY ACIDS: Help reduce inflammation, good for mood regulation and support brain health.
- **Food Sources:** fatty fish (salmon and Mackerel), flaxseeds, chia seeds, walnuts and seaweed, grass fed beef

FRUITS & VEGETABLES: Abundant with vitamins, minerals and antioxidants which are important for postpartum healing.
- **Food Sources:** berries, citrus fruits, dark leafy greens, bell peppers and carrots (Ideally cooked vegetables as they're softer and easier to digest.)

GRAINS AND STARCHES: Provide essential nutrients, fiber to aid digestion and carbohydrates for sustained energy.
- **Food Sources:** quinoa, brown rice, oats, sweet potato, potatoes, butternut squash, lentils and chickpeas

03 / PREPARING FOOD

Over the next few pages we are going to look at postpartum food prep! You don't have to do it alone mama. There are many options available to make sure you have nutritious and healthy food available. We will look at easy recipe ideas you can prepare, freezer meals, food train and there is a meal prep calendar to help you plan. Foods marked with an asterisks (*) are great for freezing.

SNACK IDEAS

Energy Balls* - good fat and protein
Macaroons* - high in fiber and coconut fat
Spinach Dip - greens, dairy and protein
Roasted Nori - said to be good for breastfeeding
Breakfast Cookies* - loaded with protein and fats
Chia Pudding - high in fiber, protein, calcium and fats

EASY BREAKFAST

Overnight Oats - good fiber and nutrients
Yogurt & Granola - provides probiotics and protein
Blender Pancakes* - they're quick and nutritious
Breakfast Burrito* - ample protein and veggies
Egg Cup* - good source of protein and carbs
Muffins* - easy to customize, nutritious, and portable

QUICK LUNCH

Buddha Bowl - very nutrient-rich and balanced
Pesto Pasta* - rich in healthy fats and filling
Avocado Toast - good fats and carbs
Turkey Chili* - high in protein and minerals
Chicken Noodle Soup* - ideal for hydration and protein
Salmon Cakes* - omega-3 fatty acids, and a source of iron

03/ POSTPARTUM MEAL PLAN

Week:

	BREAKFAST	LUNCH	DINNER
MON			
TUES			
WED			
THURS			
FRI			
SAT			
SUN			

03/ POSTPARTUM DAILY PLAN

Date:

BREAKFAST

LUNCH

DINNER

SNACKS

WATER INTAKE
💧 💧 💧 💧 💧 💧 💧 💧

GROCERY LIST

NOTES

03/ POSTPARTUM DELIVERY

Write down places you like to order grocery delivery or favorite restaurants or prepared meal boxes. This will be helpful to those supporting you if you need assistance.

GROCERY	MEAL SERVICES

Notes

WHAT'S A POSTPARTUM MEAL TRAIN?

It's an easy way for your friends and family to help you in the early days postpartum.

Have you heard of a meal train? Do you know how to ask for support with this? Do you think your friends and family would help with a meal train? Does this feel overwhelming? Let's make this an easy and fun step for everyone.

A meal train can really ease the transition into the postpartum period by ensuring you are taken care of mama. With nourishing and delicious meals. I think it's important to let those around you provide support in the early days. A time to focus on your baby and body, not what to cook for dinner.

03/ POSTPARTUM MEAL TRAIN

STEP 1
ASK A FRIEND TO LEAD THE MEAL TRAIN

STEP 2
SHARE ANY DIETARY RESTRICTIONS

STEP 3
LEADER ORGANIZES ONLINE PLATFORM

STEP 4
LEADER CREATES A SCHEDULE

STEP 5
SPREADS THE WORD TO FAMILY & FRIENDS

STEP 6
SHARE GUIDELINES (MEAL REQUESTS, ALLERGIES)

STEP 7
ENCOURAGE VARIETY

STEP 8
DELIVERY INSTRUCTIONS SHARED

STEP 9
MEALS ARE DELIVERED FROZEN OR FRESH

STEP 10
MAMA CAN FOLLOW UP WITH NOTES

MAMA CHECK IN

POSTPARTUM MEAL PLANNING

After this chapter, do you have a better idea of how you can support yourself with great food, who can step up when you don't have energy cook and when you can call on a friend to set up your meal train? Food can really support your postpartum healing and it can also be time consuming. Let's start brainstorming so you can ask for help.

What are some of your favorite foods? Write them down to share with your meal train.

_____
_____
_____
_____
_____
_____

List some delicious snack ideas you could prepare and freeze for easy on the go snacks.

_____
_____
_____
_____
_____
_____

MAMA CHECK IN

POSTPARTUM NUTRITION CHECKLIST

I was thinking it's easy to read about meal planning and nutrition but sometimes hard to put it into practice. I've prepared a Postpartum Nutrition Checklist to help set you up for success for the first weeks after birth. These are ways you can prepare before the baby arrives. You will need to ask for help, but it will be worth it!

Meal Planning To Do List

- Print off the Flourishing Postpartum Meal Plan book.

- Meal plan and prepare meals and snacks for your freezer.

- In the weekly planner then list frozen meals that can be used in the first weeks postpartum.

- Make a grocery order for delivery or pick up that is already in your cart so all you have to do is place the order. For every day items you'll need.

- Pick someone to organize the meal train. Then figure out the best day to activate the meal train. Would a week postpartum be helpful?

- If friends or family ask how they can help, ask them for a freezer meal or help with recipes for meal planning.

MAMA CHECK IN

DOWNLOAD THE MEAL PLANNER

Mama, I figured it would be easiest to have a meal planner you could download and print off. Then you will have multiple sheets for your daily and weekly meal prep. I've also included a few simple postpartum recipes like smoothies, snacks and light meals, as well as grocery list and inventory tracker. As a new mama, keeping track of what is in the pantry off the top of your head can be difficult, having a sheet where you can write items you are low on can be super helpful in postpartum.

> "NUTRITION IS THE EASIEST WAY TO SUPPORT OUR BODIES DURING POSTPARTUM."

Tijana

Chapter 04

BECOMING A MAMA

LET'S LOOK AT THE JOURNEY INTO POSTPARTUM & MOTHERHOOD

WELCOME TO MOTHERHOOD

I wasn't ready for the transition into motherhood. Pregnancy seemed liked this unfolding and I had a lot of support and information on what my body and baby were going through. Then, BAM! Motherhood and Postpartum, I felt lost. What was happening to my body? How could I support my baby?

Becoming a mama is beautiful and transformative experience. You have no idea what it holds until you've arrived. Be gentle with yourself mama as your body transitions into postpartum, you start to get to know your new baby and discover who you are as a mama. Let's look at how to heal, ways to support your sleep, how to recognize the baby blues and caring for yourself in early postpartum.

Becoming a Mama

04/ VAGINAL BIRTH

Right after birth, a woman's body will undergo changes and it begins it's postpartum recovery process. These help the body to return to it's pre-pregnancy state

Uterine Contractions: after birth the uterus contracts to expel the placenta and reduce it's size. Afterpains can be quite strong, especially when breastfeeding.

Vaginal Bleeding: Postpartum bleeding, known as lochia, happens as the body sheds it's uterine lining, plus the blood and tissue from pregnancy.

Breast Changes: They may become swollen, engorged or tender as they start to product milk.

Vaginal Changes: The are may be sore or stretched after giving birth.

Abdominal Changes: Which were stretch during pregnancy, begin to retract. The belly may still look distended but will reduce in size over the postpartum period.

Hormonal Fluctuations: Estrogen and progesterone rapidly change after birth.

04/ VAGINAL BIRTH HEALING

PAIN MEDICATION

Your healthcare provider may prescribe pain meds for discomfort. Take as prescribed, if you don't want pain medication discuss alternatives with your doctor.

ICE PACK

Using on the perineal area can help with swelling and pain relief. Use an ice pack (covered with a cloth) or a padscicle (homemade or purchased).

WARM SITZ BATH

Can promote healing and help soothe the perineal area. Fill a shallow basin with warm water and sit in it for 15 to 20 minutes a few times per day. Pat area dry.

PERINEAL CARE

Use a peri bottle with warm water to rinse after using the bathroom and gently pat dry. keep area clean and dry,

REST

Allow yourself plenty of rest to support your body's healing process. Take moments to rest or sleep when baby sleeps. Avoid overexerting yourself.

AVOID HEAVY LIFTING

This can strain the pelvic area and slow down the healing process. Take it slow and ask for help when you need it,

GENTLE MOVEMENT

Light walking and gentle movement can really help to improve circulation and promote healing. Try postpartum stretches to help with breastfeeding and holding the baby.

NUTRITION

Food is such an important piece to healing postpartum. Nutritious foods help support your body's healing, breastfeeding journey and energy. Plus, drinking lots of water is important.

HYDRATION

Is needed to prevent dehydration after labor and birth, Hydration also supports healing, by helping your body repair any tissue damage. Lastly hydration is good for preventing constipation.

04/ CESAREAN BIRTH

After a cesarean birth the physical changes are very different than a vaginal birth. The recovery can be more due to the surgery.

Incision: The biggest change is the incision on your lower abdomen to deliver the baby. Usually closed with stitches or staples. Covered with gauze in the early days.

Abdominal Pain: Soreness or discomfort around the incision site. Normal to feel tenderness and sensitivity in the area. Possible numbness as well.

Less Mobile: Limited due to the abdominal incision. Can be hard to move, walk or get out of bed. May need assistance getting up.

Hospital Stay: Can be longer with a c-section to monitor mama's recovery and incision.

Catheter & IV Lines: Used during a c-section for monitoring and providing fluids/medications. They are usually removed a few days after the cesarean.

Bowel Movement: May be delayed or take longer to return to normal.

Lifting Limited: Mamas usually advised not to life heavy objects or do any strenuous activities. Baby is fine to lift.

Pain Management: Pain meds prescribed to manage pain and discomfort.

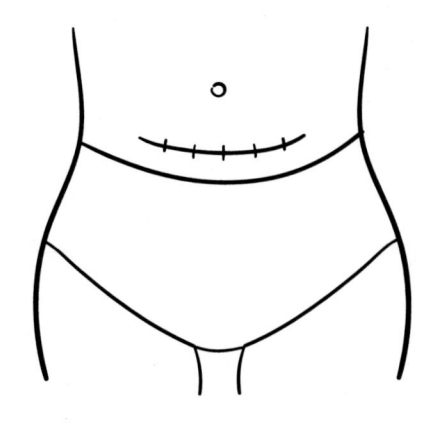

04/ CESAREAN BIRTH HEALING

PAIN MEDICATION

Your healthcare provider may prescribe pain meds to manage surgery discomfort. Be sure to stay on the pain management schedule.

INCISION CARE

Important to keep the incision area clean and dry. Watch for any signs of infection, such as swelling, redness or discharge. Cold packs can also help with swelling or discomfort.

SCAR MASSAGE

Be sure to wait until your incision has healed. Once healed, gently massage scar with vitamin E oil or silicone-based gel. A pelvic floor therapist can help with this or find massages online.

SUPPORTIVE PILLOWS

Good to use when lying down or sitting to reduce pressure on the incision area. The pillows are also helpful for getting up and down or when laughing or sneezing,

REST

Allow yourself plenty of rest to support your body's healing process. Take moments to rest or sleep when baby sleeps. Avoid overexerting yourself.

AVOID HEAVY LIFTING

Avoid any heavy lifting during the early weeks postpartum. When lifting your baby or other objects be sure to use proper technique. You want to avoid straining your belly muscles.

GENTLE MOVEMENT

Light walking can help prevent blood clots and improve circulation. This will help the healing process. Start with short walks and increase as you feel better.

NUTRITION

Food is such an important to piece to healing postpartum. Nutritious foods help support your body's healing, breastfeeding journey and energy. Plus, drinking lots of water is important.

HYDRATION

Helps the body heal from the physical stress of surgery. Hydration promotes faster healing and can prevent infection. Hydration can prevent constipation which can be uncomfortable after a cesarean birth.

04/ BABY BLUES VS PPD

BABY BLUES

Experienced by most new mamas, typically emerge within the first week after birth and will resolve within two weeks.

- Mood Swings: Feeling happy one moment and tearful the next, from hormonal changes

- Tearfulness: Crying spells without a clear trigger may occur. You may have tears and not know why.

- Fatigue & Anxiety: Feeling overwhelmed, anxious and exhausted.

- Sensitivity: Insignificant events might cause reactions that are out of proportion.

PPD

A more severe condition affecting some new mamas. Typically emerges within the first few weeks or months after childbirth.

- Ongoing Sadness: A deep feeling of sadness or hopelessness. Lasting weeks or months.

- Irritability or Anger: Intense irritability, angry outbursts or overwhelming frustration.

- Bonding with Baby: Feeling detached from the baby or not forming an emotional conenction.

- Loss of interest: A decrease in enjoyment of activities or feeling disconnected from others.

It is important to understand the difference between baby blues and perinatal mood and anxiety disorders (PMAD's) which is a term used to refer to mental health disorders during pregnancy, after giving birth or adopting. Postpartum Depression (PPD) is often used as an umbrella term but PMAD's include, anxiety, bipolar disorder, psychosis, depression, PTSD and Obsessive-compulsive disorder (OCD). Please make sure yourself and support team are familiar with the symptoms.

04/ BREAST CHANGES

Let's look at what happens for your breasts following the birth of your baby. Every feeding journey is unique, here's a little of what to expect.

Engorgement
- Occurs when breasts swell
- Feel firm and hard
- A few days after birth
- Can be uncomfortable

↓

Colostrum
- First few days post birth
- A nutrient-rich, thick and yellow fluid, serves as baby's first milk
- Provides antibodies & nutrients

↓

Tenderness
- Can have sensitivity
- Possible mild pain
- Related to hormonal changes and increased flow to breast tissue

↓

04/ BREAST CHANGES

Don't be worried about all of these breast changes. Once you and your baby find your feeding rhythm then your breasts will find their "flow".

Leaking Milk

- Common for breasts to leak
- When baby cries
- During the milk letdown
- Nursing pads can be helpful

↓

Letdown

- Feeling of tingling
- Sensation of pins & needles
- Happens during breastfeeding or when baby cries

↓

Nipple Changes

- May be more sensitive
- Can appear flattened
- Could be elongated after feedings
- May require nipple cream for dryness

↓

04/ BREAST CHANGES

Let's look at what happens for mama and baby after birth. This covers the postpartum period or fourth trimester from 24 hours to 6 months.

Cluster Feeding

- Early days postpartum
- Frequent and intense feeding
- Totally normal
- Stimulates milk production

↓

Size Changes

- Fluctuates in early postpartum
- Size settles after a few weeks
- Breasts will be larger during breastfeeding

04/ FEEDING YOUR BABY

Mama, how to feed your baby is entirely your choice. Everyone will have an opinion, you need to do what's right for your body, baby and family. This is no one else's choice to make. Let's look at some ways you can feed your baby.

- BREASTFEED
- FORMULA FEED
- PUMP AND BOTTLE FEED EXPRESSED MILK
- COMBINATION FEED BREASTFEED AND FORMULA
- BREASTFEED AND BOTTLE FEED EXPRESSED MILK
- MAMA THIS IS YOUR JOURNEY AND YOU KNOW WHAT'S BEST FOR YOU AND YOUR BABY

04/ FEEDING YOUR BABY

Sometimes you will need to supplement. If you are wanting to breastfeed then I would focus on that, but if you are struggling with low milk supply, medical issues or a baby struggling to feed.

Options for Supplementation

01. Expressed breast milk from newborns parent

02. Donor breast milk

03. Protein hydrolysate formulas

04. Consult primary care for other supplement options

04/ THE 5-5-5 RULE

After giving birth allowing your body to rest is important for your wellbeing, recovery and long-term health. Most new mamas underestimate their body's need for recovery. Aim for at least 15 days of dedicated recovery time after your birth. Here's how to divide it up!

	what to do	*what not to do*	*partner's role*
FIRST FIVE DAYS: *in the bed*	• Spend 100% of your time resting in bed or on the couch • Nap or sleep as much as you can • Focus on feeding & bonding • Lots of skin to skin sessions • Limit (or avoid) visitors • Sitz baths for perineal healing • Lots of water and healthy meals	• Invite lots of visitors/host visits longer than 30 minutes • Household chores, laundry, cooking, pet care • Walks around the block/store • Be in a rush to wean off post-birth medications • Make plans for more than 3 days in advance	• Provide meals, snacks, and water bottle refills • Take care of household chores, pet care, and older siblings • Run errands • Diaper changes and burping • Remind partner to take pain relief medication • Ask visitors to leave when time
NEXT FIVE DAYS: *on the bed*	• Spend 75% of your time resting in bed or on the couch (90 minutes of rest for 30 minutes of activity) • Stay in your pajamas to keep yourself in "rest mode" • Sit outside for fresh air • Begin inviting visitors if you're ready	• Rush your recovery. If you're starting to feel better, it means resting is working- keep doing it • Housework, chores, cooking • Long drives/outings • Limit skin-to-skin access • Feel pressured to have visitors	• Remind your partner to continue resting • Provide meals and snacks • Give your partner time to process/debrief from the birth • Provide emotional support • Help your partner get to/from doctor's appointments
LAST FIVE DAYS: *near the bed*	• Spend 50% of your time resting in bed or on the couch (60 minutes of rest for 60 minutes of activity) • Short walks around the block are okay, but stay near your bed • Craft projects, reading, movie marathons, puzzles, etc • Limit chores to things like folding laundry from the couch	• Over-exert yourself (more bleeding means too much activity) • Long drives/outings • Walking around the store or mall • Housework, chores, pet care, errands • Visiting at other people's homes (let them come to you)	• Meal and snack prep for when you return to work • Make sure your partner is getting at least 2 hours uninterrupted sleep at a time • Ensure your partner doesn't take on too much activity too soon • Accompany your partner on walks and outings

04/ EMOTIONAL CARE

SEEK SUPPORT
REACH OUT TO FAMILY AND FRIENDS TO CONNECT

PARTNER CONNECTION
COMMUNICATE ABOUT CHALLENGES OR EMOTIONS

REST AND SELF-CARE
LOTS OF REST, ACTIVITIES FOR JOY & SELF-COMPANSSION

MINFULNESS & RELAXATION
DEEP BREATHING & RELAXATION TO REDUCE ANXIETY & STRESS

STAY NOURISHED
STAY HYDRATED & EAT NUTRITIOUS MEALS FOR YOUR WELL-BEING

MANAGE EXPECTATIONS
IT'S OK TO ASK FOR HELP & TAKE TIME TO ADJUST TO MOTHERHOOD

LIMIT SOCIAL MEDIA
AVOID COMPARISSION & THE NEED TO MEET CERTAIN STANDARDS

ACCEPT HELP
LET OTHERS HELP WITH HOUSEHOLD TASKS, FOOD OR OLDER KIDS

TIME FOR BONDING
SKIN-TO-SKIN CONTACT & QUALITY TIME WITH BABY

PPMDS
BE AWARE SIGNS OF DEPRESSION, ANXIETY OR OTHER MOOD DISORDERS

04/ SUPPORTING YOUR SLEEP

Sleep deprivation in early postpartum can be challenging for both parents. There are ways you can support your body and manage fatigue. Here are some ways you can help yourself through sleep deprivation. Remember the newborn phase is short and their sleep will soon become more predictable. Make sure you create a plan to support your sleep.

NAP WHEN BABY SLEEPS

I know this is not always easy! If you're able to use your baby's naptime to rest or catch up on sleep, it can be so rejuvenating.

SHARE NIGHTTIME

If you're able to take turns with your partner during night feeds or diaper changes to create rest for both of you. Then both parents can get some uninterrupted sleep.

ACCEPT HELP

Let family or friends help with household chores or meals. Always say yes when someone offers help!

PRIORITIZE SLEEP

Try to go to bed at the same time each night and make sure it's early. If you can't get a full night's sleep, going to bed earlier with help increase the amount of sleep.

NIGHTTIME ROUTINE

Having a relaxing bedtime routine can signal to your body that it's time o wind down and prepare for sleep. This saved me in early postpartum

SLEEP IN SHIFTS

With your partner or a family member or doula create a sleep schedule. One person can care for the baby while the other one sleeps and then switch.

SLEEP SPACE

A room that's dark and quiet, ready for sleep. Use blackout curtains, white noise, earplugs or an eye mask to block out disruptions. Plus then you can sleep day or night.

STAY HYDRATED

Did you know dehydration can increase feelings of fatigue and in some cases create insomnia symptoms. Drink lots of water during the day. Make sure you track it.

LIMIT CAFFEINE

Try not to reply on coffee or tea to provide energy or to stay awake. This can disrupt your sleep patterns. Obviously have a cup in the morning! You need to get through the day mama!

04/ POSTPARTUM HAIR LOSS

Postpartum hair loss is a common condition that occurs for many mamas after birth. This means an excessive shedding or loss of hair, that typically starts around 2 to 4 months after childbirth. Mamas can feel concerned, but it's natural and temporary phase.

what to expect

INCREASED HAIR SHEDDING: You may notice more hair falling out than usual. Especially when brushing or showering.

THINNING HAIR: As the hair sheds more than usual you may notice thinning around the scalp.

WIDENING PART: Mamas with long hair may notice their part is thinning. One note from my hairdresser is to change your part to relieve the hair stress.

BABY BANGS: Some mamas may have regrowth of hair around the hairline. Often referred to as "baby bangs" which are short, wispy hairs.

hair loss tips

BE GENTLE WITH YOUR HAIR: If you can avoid hair treatments or styles that involve a lot of heat or add stress to the hair like a tight ponytail.

MAINTAIN A HEALTHY DIET: A balanced diet rich in vitamins and minerals can support hair health. Foods such as almonds, eggs, strawberries, dark leafy greens, and oily fish.

TAKE CARE OF YOUR SCALP: Keeping the scalp clean and moisturized can promote a healthy environment for hair growth.

CONSIDER YOUR HAIR CARE PRODUCTS: If you have some hair loss, products such as volumizing shampoos and conditioners could help give an appearance of fuller hair.

PATIENCE: Remember, postpartum hair loss is temporary and the hair usually regrows on its own, with time.

MAMA CHECK IN

TAKE A MOMENT

Mama, I know this chapter is a doozy! It's not meant to scare you but PREPARE you! Knowing how you can support your sleep, emotional well-being, healing and feeding your baby. Let's take a few moments to write down how you are feeling.

When you think about your feeding journey, what comes up? We will create a bigger plan in Chapter 7.

_____
_____
_____
_____
_____
_____
_____

Who could help you with your emotional care and sleep?

_____
_____
_____
_____
_____
_____
_____

POSTPARTUM PLAN

CREATE A POSTPARTUM
BATHROOM BOX TO HELP YOU IN
EARLY POSTPARTUM

- [ ] Bathroom Basket
- [ ] Perineal Care Products
- [ ] Perineal Spray
- [ ] Witch Hazel Pads
- [ ] Maxi Pads (for Postpartum)
- [ ] Disposable Underwear
- [ ] Stool Softeners
- [ ] Nursing Pads (Reusable are great!)
- [ ] Nipple Cream
- [ ] Perineal Ice Packs
- [ ] Water Bottle with Straw
- [ ] Essential Oils

POSTPARTUM PLAN

MAKE A PLAN

Mama, let's write out a nightly routine. This is something that saved me in early postpartum. It can be something simple like a cup of tea, applying some moisturizer or getting anything you need for night feedings.

_____
_____
_____
_____
_____
_____
_____
_____
_____
_____
_____
_____
_____
_____
_____
_____
_____

POSTPARTUM PLAN

YOUR 5-5-5 PLAN

In creating a 5-5-5 plan you need support. Who could that be for you? Your partner, grandparent, friend or postpartum doula? How will you get the rest you need in early postpartum?

_____
_____
_____
_____
_____
_____
_____
_____
_____
_____
_____
_____
_____
_____
_____
_____
_____
_____

"BECOMING A MAMA IS LIKE GOING ON A JOURNEY WITHOUT A MAP. TRUST IF YOU HAVE THE RIGHT SUPPORT, YOU WILL FIND YOUR WAY."

Tijana

Chapter 05

SUPPORTING BABY

LETS GET TO KNOW YOUR NEWBORN AND WHAT THEY NEED BEFORE THEY ARRIVE.

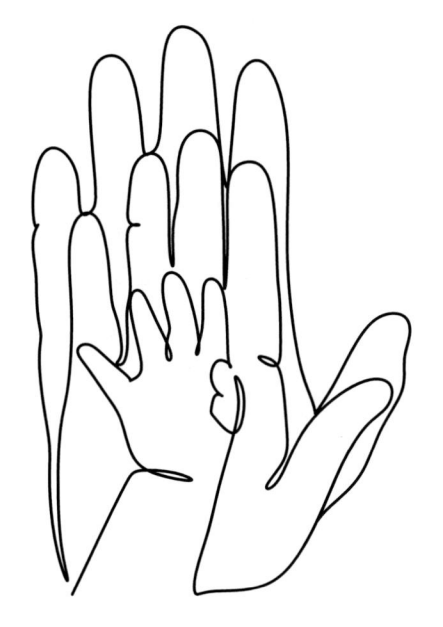

GETTING TO KNOW YOUR BABY

Besides some tips on breastfeeding my prenatal class didn't cover much more about newborns. I think having an idea of a newborn's sleep, feeding and newborn care before the baby arrives is a great idea. You might not remember it all but will be able to reference your postpartum plan and all my notes about newborns.

Do you know where your baby will sleep? How long newborns sleep? What type of feeding position will work for you? How to store breastmilk? What about bathing a newborn? Or how to make a newborn comfortable? Let's review all of this and more. Then you can make know how best to care for your newborn baby.

Learn about Newborns

05/ SAFE SLEEP OPTIONS

There are many options available for your newborn baby to sleep in. Let's look at the safest places and why they are a good option.

safe sleep

CRIB: A crib is a safe sleep option for babies. It provides a firm and flat sleep surface. Make sure to use a snug-fitting crib mattress with a fitted sheet.

BASSINET: A bassinet is a smaller sleep option suitable for newborns and younger babies. It provides a cozy and secure sleep environment. Choose a bassinet with a firm, flat mattress and a fitted sheet.

PLAY YARD WITH BASSINET ATTACHMENT: Some play yards have a detachable bassinet feature. Please be sure to follow the weight and size restrictions.

CO-SLEEPER OR BEDSIDE SLEEPER: A co-sleeper or beside sleeper attaches to the parents bed or sits close to the bedside. It allows for easy access to the baby during the night for comforting and easy feeding.

TRAVEL CRIB: A portable or travel crib is a great option for families on the go. Make sure to choose a firm mattress and fitted sheet.

PLEASE NOTE: Rock'n'Plays, Swings or Car Seats are not advised for routine sleep according to the American Academy of Pediatrics (AAP). These devices are not designed for safe sleep and can pose risks to your baby.

sleep guidelines

BACK TO SLEEP: Always place the baby on their back for sleep for naps and nighttime.

FIRM SLEEP SURFACE: Avoid soft surfaces, pillows or couches for sleep. Use a firm, flat sleep surface to prevent suffocation.

NO LOOSE BEDDING OR SOFT OBJECTS: Keep sleep area free of loose bedding, blankets, pillows and stuffed animals.

AVOID OVERHEATING: Keep the room at a comfortable temperature and avoid overdressing baby for sleep.

05 / NEWBORN SLEEP

Newborns have different sleep patterns than adults. Their sleep often includes frequent wakings for feeding and comfort. On average newborns sleep for about 16 to 20 hours per day. Their sleep is divided into multiple short periods. Let's review newborn sleep so you are prepared for those early days.

SLEEP CYCLES

Newborns have shorter sleep cycles compared to adults. Their sleep cycles last around 45 minutes to an hour. They cycle through lighter and deeper sleep stages more frequently.

IRREGULAR SLEEP

Newborns do not have a fixed sleep-wake schedule. They sleep and wake up at irregular intervals throughout the day and night.

SHORT AWAKE PERIODS

Newborns only stay awake for brief periods. Usually lasting 1 to 2 hours before becoming tired and needing sleep again.

FEEDING & SLEEP

Newborns wake frequently to feed. Their small stomachs require regular feedings. They may sleep 2 to 4 hours between feedings, both day and night.

DAY-NIGHT CONFUSION

Some newborns have a hard time distinguishing between day and night. This may lead to extended periods of wakefulness during the night.

SLEEP ENVIRONMENT

Do you best to create a soothing and safe sleep environment. A calm and dark room that is comfortable temperature can help promote better sleep.

NAPPING

Newborns may take multiple short naps throughout the day. Usually naps will range from 30 minutes to 2 hours in length.

GRADUAL SLEEP CHANGES

A newborns sleep pattern will gradually change. Around three or four months, newborns will begin to develop a more predictable sleep patterns.

IMPORTANT TO REMEMBER

Every newborn is different and sleep patterns can vary from one baby to another. As a new parent be flexible and responsive to your baby.

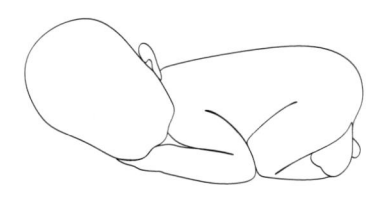

05/ NEWBORN SLEEP CUES

Newborns often display subtle sleepy cues letting you know they need rest. Recognizing these clues can help you respond to your baby's sleep needs promptly. Let's look at some common sleep cutes to watch for with your newborn. In the beginning when you are getting to know your baby you may miss the early clues, that's ok mama. Slowly you will see the cues.

I'M TIRED

- The stare
- Flushed brows
- Looks away

I'M READY FOR A NAP

- Fussiness
- Big Yawns
- Rubs Eyes

I'M OVERTIRED

- Frantic Crying
- Rigid Body
- Pushes Away

05 / BREASTFEEDING TIPS

Mama, if you choose to breastfeed your baby, you'll both have a bit to learn. Understanding what a good latch looks like. That a newborn baby needs to feed frequently. It's important to take care of yourself, breastfeeding can be demanding. Remember to take care of yourself, trust your body and your baby breastfeeding can take time for you to find your rhythm.

ESTABLISH A GOOD LATCH: A proper latch is important for successful breastfeeding. It allows your baby to effectively get milk. Plus prevents discomfort for both you and your baby. To achieve a good latch, ensure that your baby's mouth is wide open with lips flanged outward. Bring your baby to your breast, aiming the nipple towards the roof of their mouth. Watch for signs of swallowing and listen for a rhythmic sucking pattern. If you're unsure about the latch, seek help from a lactation consultant who can provide hands-on guidance. I found this to be invaluable.

NURSE FREQUENTLY & ON DEMAND:
Newborn babies have small stomachs and need to nurse frequently, usually every 2 to 3 hours. It's important to nurse your baby on demand, following their hunger cues rather than a strict schedule. Look for signs of hunger such as rooting, sucking motions, or hand-to-mouth. By nursing frequently, you establish a good milk supply and help your baby receive the nourishment they need. Keep in mind that frequent nursing is normal in the early weeks and doesn't necessarily mean you have a low milk supply.

TAKE CARE OF YOURSELF: Breastfeeding can be demanding, so self-care is so important. Stay hydrated by drinking plenty of water throughout the day, breastfeeding can increase your thirst. Eat a well-balanced diet to provide your body with the nutrients it needs for milk production. Rest whenever possible and try to nap when your baby sleeps. Seek support from your partner, family, or friends to help with household chores or baby care. Allowing you to focus on breastfeeding and self-care. Remember, taking care of yourself is essential for your well-being and the success of your breastfeeding journey.

05/ BREASTFEEDING POSITIONS

Have you ever thought to practice breastfeeding positions BEFORE the baby arrives? If this is your first baby and you've never breastfed before, it might be a good idea to sit in your nursing chair or get our your breastfeeding pillow. Sit down for a moment and practice the breastfeeding positions below. You can use a doll or stuffed animal.

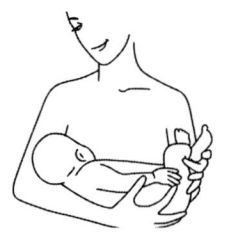

The cradle hold is one of the most common positions for breastfeeding. To do this, sit in a comfortable chair or use a nursing pillow to support your baby's weight. Hold your baby's head in the crook of your arm on the same side as the breast you're nursing from. Your baby's body should be facing you, with their nose aligned with your nipple.

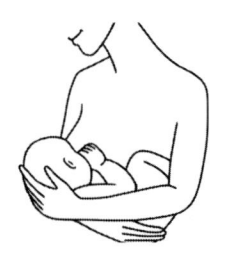

Similar to the cradle hold, the cross-cradle hold offers more support for your baby's head and neck. Hold your baby's head in the crook of the opposite arm from the breast you're nursing from. Use your other hand to support your breast and guide your baby's latch. This position is often helpful for newborns or babies who need extra support.

The football hold, also known as the clutch or underarm hold, can be helpful for mamas who have had a cesarean section or those with larger breasts. Sit in a comfortable chair and tuck your baby's body under your arm on the same side as the breast you're nursing from. Support your baby's head with your hand, and their body will be positioned along the side of your body, facing your breast.

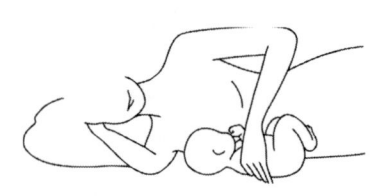

The side-lying position can be particularly useful during night feedings or when you want to rest while breastfeeding. Lie on your side with your baby facing you, tummy to tummy. Use a nursing pillow or rolled-up blanket to support your baby's body and bring them closer to your breast. This position allows you to relax while nursing.

In the laid-back position, also known as biological nurturing, you recline slightly and allow your baby to lie on top of you, nestled against your body. Use gravity to help your baby find their latch naturally. This position can be helpful for newborns and babies who may have difficulty latching in other positions.

PAGE 72

05 / NEWBORN HUNGER CUES

Crying is not the only hunger cue, there are many small things your baby may do to show you they are hungry. Every baby is different. In the early days of postpartum get to know your baby's hunger cues and how they show you they are ready to feed.

EARLY HUNGER CUES

- Stirring, moving arms
- Mouth opening, yawning or licking
- Hand to mouth
- Turning head side to side
- Rooting, reach with mouth

MID HUNGER CUES

- Stretching
- Moving more and more
- Hand to mouth
- Sucking or cooing sounds

LATE HUNGER CUES

- Crying
- Agitated body movements
- Turning red

05 / BREAST MILK STORAGE

	fresh EXPRESSED OR PUMPED	*thawed* PREVIOUSLY FROZEN
ROOM TEMP 77° F/25° C or colder	up to 4 HOURS	up to 4 HOURS
COOLER with ice packs	up to 24 HOURS	up to 24 HOURS
REFRIGERATOR 40° F/4° C	up to 4 DAYS	up to 24 HOURS
FREEZER 0° F/-18° C	up to 6 MONTHS	NEVER refreeze thawed milk
FREEZER 0° F/-18° C	up to 12 MONTHS	NEVER refreeze thawed milk

TIPS

- If baby doesn't finish bottle use that milk within 2 hours.
- Never rewarm previously warmed breastmilk.
- Freeze in small amounts of 2 to 4 ounces to avoid waste.
- Clearly label breast milk with the date it was expressed.

05 / LACTATION COOKIE RECIPE

The lactation cookie, a popular choice among breastfeeding mamas, as they often contain ingredients believed to support milk production. As a new mama the lactation cookie was my go to snack! I loved the taste, texture and energy they provided. If you need a simple snack to support your body postpartum and that you can easily freeze, lactation cookies are the answer!

1.5 cups old fashioned oats
1 cup all-purpose flour
1/2 cup whole wheat flour
1/2 cup ground flaxseed
1/2 cup brewers yeast
1 tsp baking powder
1/2 tsp baking soda
1/2 tsp salt

1/2 cup unsalted butter, softened
1/2 cup coconut oil
1 cup brown sugar
2 large eggs
1 tsp vanilla extract
1 cup dark chocolate chips or raisins
1/2 cup chopped nuts (almonds or walnuts

1. Preheat your oven to 350°F (175°C) and line a baking sheet with parchment paper.
2. In a large mixing bowl, combine the oats, all-purpose flour, whole wheat flour, ground flaxseed, brewer's yeast, baking powder, baking soda, and salt. Set aside.
3. In another bowl, cream together the softened butter, coconut oil, and brown sugar until light and fluffy.
4. Add the eggs and vanilla extract to the butter mixture and mix well.
5. Gradually add the dry ingredient mixture to the wet ingredients and mix until well combined.
6. If desired, fold in the dark chocolate chips or raisins and chopped nuts.
7. Scoop rounded tablespoons of the dough onto the prepared baking sheet, spacing them about 2 inches apart.
8. Bake for 10-12 minutes or until the edges are lightly golden.
9. Remove from the oven and let the cookies cool on the baking sheet for a few minutes before transferring them to a wire rack to cool completely.
10. Enjoy your delicious lactation cookie! Store them in an airtight container for up to a week or freeze for longer storage.

05/ BREASTFEEDING TRACKER

Date: _____

DATE	BREAST LEFT	BREAST RIGHT	FEEDING DURATION	BABY'S MOOD

DIAPER

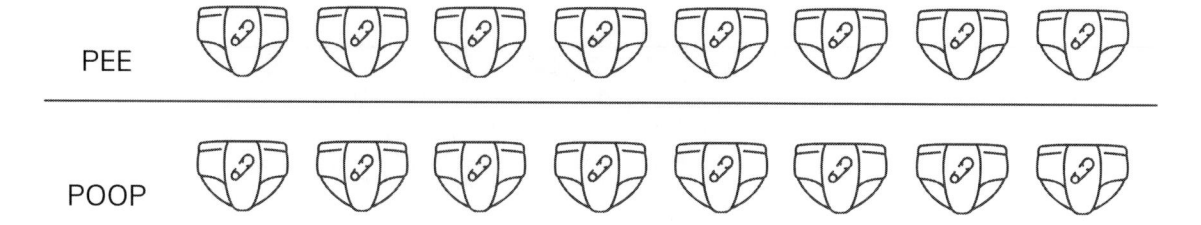

PEE

POOP

05/ SOOTHING A NEWBORN

In the first trimester you may find your baby will cry without reason and you may have difficulty soothing them. Here are some ways you can support you baby. Sometimes nothing will soothe a newborn. Make sure you have support during this time to help with comforting the baby and giving you a break mama!

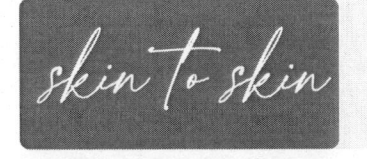

skin to skin — When your baby can hear your heartbeat, feel your warmth and sense mama's presence, it helps their nervous system relax. Skin to skin also helps with bonding for mama and baby.

swaddle — Swaddling can help mimic the tight quarters of the womb. It's worth learning how to swaddle. Ask your nurse in the hospital or doula how to safely swaddle your baby.

shush — The shush should be as loud as your babies cry. You could shush using your own voice, a noise machine or app. These noises remind your baby of the womb and offer comfort.

swing — Every movement in the womb rocked our baby. When they're crying You want to gently jiggle your baby, not fully swing. Ideally while you're shushing. Or you can walk around with them in a baby wrap.

suck — Babies find sucking very soothing. You can let the baby suck your finger, a soother or offer another feeding session. Our one twin liked the soother, but our other daughter naturally sucked without one.

step away — If you've tried everything and your baby is still crying, mama you've done nothing wrong. At this point it would be good to take a break, place your baby down and ask your partner, a friend or family member for help.

05 / BATHING A NEWBORN

Bathing a newborn can be a wonderful bonding experience. In the early days it's gentle and quiet, a slow way to end a day. Let's look at how to bath a newborn safely.

1. GATHER SUPPLIES: clean soft towel, baby soap, clean diaper, washcloth and basin of warm water.

2. SAFE LOCATION: baby bath tub or flat surface. have all supplies within reach.

3. UNDRESS BABY: take off all clothes, then supporting the head & neck slowly lower them into the bath.

4. WASH BABY: use a soft washcloth & small amount of soap. clean face, body, folds of skin & hair.

5. RINSE: using a small cup or your hands, make sure there is no soap residue left on your baby's skin.

6. WRAP & DRY: wrap baby in a soft towel and gently pat dry, making sure to get the skin folds.

TIPS

- Never leave baby unattended during the bath.
- Only fill the basin or baby tub with a few inches of water.
- Always support your baby's head and neck during bath time.

05/ DIAPERING YOUR BABY

Mama, when was the last time you put a diaper on a baby? You will soon be a pro! Sometimes it takes a few tries to find the right diaper for your baby. Let's look at a few things you should know before your baby arrives.

TYPES OF DIAPERS

You have two choices when it comes to diapers, disposable or cloth. It's what works for you and your family.

DIAPER SIZES

They come in many sizes. You'll need to switch sizes as they grow. Leaking diapers are usually a sign they are too small.

DIAPER CHANGES

Newborns need frequent diaper changes. Most likely 8 to 12 times per day. Make sure your change table is stocked daily.

IS IT WET?

It's a good idea to check your baby's diaper regularly to see if it's wet or soiled. Keeping your baby clean and dry will prevent diaper rash & discomfort.

DIAPER RASH

Promptly change baby's diaper when wet/soiled. Use a diaper cream or ointment when needed to create a barrier on their skin.

DIAPER SUPPLIES

Stock your change table with diapers, wipes, diaper cream & changing pad. If possible have two changing stations set up in your home.

HOW TO WIPE

Be gentle when wiping during diaper changes and always wipe from front to back to prevent infections.

OVERNIGHT DIAPERS

These can handle more wetness and helps prevent leaks and discomfort for you baby.

TRAVELING

Whether it's a trip to the store or a road trip make sure you always have your diaper supplies. Plus plastic bags for dirty diapers & changing pad.

DIAPER PAIL

Use these next to your change table. They store soiled diapers and prevent odors as they have a tight sealing lid.

DIAPER BUDGET

They are an ongoing expense. It's good to consider the cost, add it to your monthly budget & look for sales. 10 diapers per day is 300 a month!

DIAPER BRANDS

Each brand has a different fit and it's a good idea to try a few to find one that works for your baby. We tried 3 brands before we found a good fit.

05/ BABY'S FIRST DAYS

Rather than relying on your feedings, look at your baby's diaper to make sure they are getting enough milk. Remember your baby will feed 8 to 12 times in 24 hours, that's every 1.5 to 3 hours. Feeds will last anywhere from 20 to 60 minutes.

	bowel movements	*wet diapers*
DAYS 1 TO 3	1 - 3 MECONIUM	1 TO 3 INCREASING
DAYS 3 TO 4	3 TO 4 BROWN/YELLOW	3 TO 4 HEAVIER
DAYS 5 TO 6	3 TO 5 YELLOW	5 TO 6 HEAVY WET

Mama, I think it can be easy to obsess over feedings and whether your baby is getting enough in the early days. Use this chart when in doubt. The diapers will always tell you if your baby is getting enough milk.

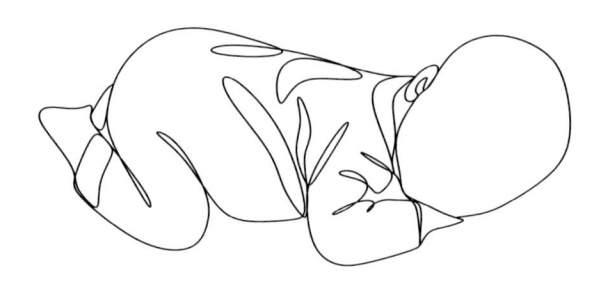

POSTPARTUM PLAN

LET'S PLAN

Getting to know your newborn will happen over time, but it's great to understand their sleep cycles, bowel movements, and feeding.

Where will your newborn sleep? During the day and in the evening? Will you have different areas?

Example: We had bassinets in the living room for day & a side sleeper in the bedroom for night.

_____
_____
_____
_____
_____
_____

Do you have everything for your baby's bath time? Ideally keep everything together so you know where it is.

- Soft washcloth.
- A place to wash your baby (baby bath, basin, large sink)
- Baby soap
- Soft towel.
- A diaper supply in the bathroom.

POSTPARTUM PLAN

LET'S PLAN

Getting to know your newborn will happen over time, but it's great to understand their sleep cycles, bowel movements, and feedings.

Are you planning on breastfeeding? Have you practiced different holds?

_____
_____
_____
_____
_____
_____
_____

What can you do to help prepare for your newborn before they arrive?

Example: Bake Lactation Cookies or Take Picture of Milk Storage page.

_____
_____
_____
_____
_____
_____
_____

"AS A MAMA YOU DISCOVER A LOVE YOU NEVER KNEW EXISTED, WRAPPED UP IN SLEEPLESS NIGHTS, CHALLENGES AND CUDDLES."

Tijana

Chapter

06

FAMILY EDUCATION

MAKING SURE EVERYONE IS ON THE SAME PAGE AND KNOWS HOW TO SUPPORT YOUR FAMILY

MAKING A FAMILY PLAN

If everyone in your family knows how they can support you, your boundaries around visiting hours, the help you need with older children and what sleep might look like, then there are no surprises. As a mama I had to set a boundary with my brother in early postpartum. Evie and Poppy were in the NICU and they showed up with sick kids. On the pediatricians recommendation, no one was able to go into the NICU, due to the risk. My brother hasn't spoken to me since.

Setting aside this time to discuss visitors, boundaries, self-care, sibling support and more with your partner is SO VALUABLE. Having the discussion before the baby arrives means you're both on the same page and can step in if needed to set boundaries or help each other.

Let's start setting some boundaries

06/ BOUNDARIES WITH VISITORS

Postpartum boundaries are vital to creating the environment you wish for in postpartum. This chapter is meant to be discussed with your partner so you can create clear and respectful rules for all.

EXPECTATIONS FOR VISITORS AND FAMILY

- **Communicate in Advance:** Touch base with visitors before the baby arrives or prior to a visit

- **Visiting Hours:** Yes you can let family and friends know the feeding and sleep schedule and times that are convenient.

- **Small Groups:** Consider limiting the number of visitors at a time. To keep a calm and comfortable space.

- **Photography & Social Media:** Let family & friends know your preferences with sharing photos.

- **Your Needs First:** The mama and baby's well-being is most important and visits can be cut short due to eithers needs.

- **Hospital Visits;** No one has to visit you in the hospital. This is entirely your choice. After birth is a sacred time for a family. Choose what's right for you.

- **No Drop-Ins:** Request that visitors notify you before coming over. This makes sure you are able to accept visitors and are prepared.

- **Feeding Choices:** You get to choose what is right for you and set boundaries around anyone who is not respectful of your choices.

It's a lot to think about, but by doing so, your partner and you will be on the same page. The boundaries will be clear. Everyone will know what to expect before the baby arrives. Communication is key, if you share your boundaries with family and friends in a respectful and clear manner, it starts a positive dialogue for all.

06 / BOUNDARIES WITH VISITORS

Having boundaries with visitors is so important. Knowing what you need help with, your visiting hours, and the expectations you have are key to good visitor experiences.

- Set & share that you that you will have visiting hours.

- You do not need to be a hostess.

- Ask visitors to wash their hands when they arrive.

- No one has to hold the baby. It's your choice.

- Cancel visits if you no longer feel up to having guests.

- Visitors can be asked to help out. Post a to do list on the wall.

06/ GRANDPARENTS ROLE

Grandparents play a special role when the baby arrives. Every family dynamic is different and you need to clearly share your expectations. Think of how often you want them at your home, what kind of support you need from them and how they can help you through your postpartum period.

Emotional Support: If the grandparents can offer emotional support to new parents as they navigate the joys and challenges of becoming parents, that's wonderful. Perhaps the grandparents in your life will not and how will you set boundaries around protecting yourself.

Babysitting: Are they able to help with older children or if this is your first baby, can they come over when you need a shower or to run errands? Discuss with them prior to the birth what works in terms of them assisting you in this area.

Bonding with Baby: It's a beautiful bond that grandparents and baby's have. It can be a loving relationship. That doesn't mean grandparents can pop by every day or expect to hold their grandchild all the time. You set the rules mama.

Help with Household Chores: Grandparents can lend a helping hand with things like laundry, tidying up, grocery shopping or other small tasks. These may seem simple but in early postpartum they can be a big relief.

06 / SIBLING SUPPORT

Welcoming another child into your family is magical! This can be a wonderful time but also a big change for everyone. Let's look at some tools to help your older child become a great big brother or sister to the new baby. Plus navigate all the big emotions that come along with the new role.

REPLAY:
baby years

- Show your older child photos and videos of them as a baby. When they were in the hospital, having a diaper change, feeding, or playing with you. Tell your child how they were as a baby, how excited you were to have them and what you loved about your time together when they were little.
- After the baby comes home verbalize these things you did for them as a baby "Did you know when you were a baby you liked to be held like this or you used to enjoy sleeping like this or you liked it when I tickled your toes" that way they can begin to understand they were once a baby and had the attention as well.

WAIT:
ask the baby

- So often we tell the older child to wait or that you're with the baby, in an article by a child psychologist they suggested changing the language, ask the baby to wait.

Examples:
- You put the baby down, then say, "Ok baby, I am going to play with your brother/sister, you wait here."
- If the baby starts to cry in the middle of dinner or an interaction with the older child say, "Sorry baby, you need to wait for me to be done with your brother/sister." (Let's be honest it will be seconds but could make a big difference.)

HELP:
with baby

- Showing your older child how he can help with the baby or entertain them.

Examples:
- Teach them how to put on the baby socks or something simple.
- When the baby's upset, maybe ask them to sing a fun song and if the baby stops crying, praise your older child for the great song and point out how happy the baby is.
- Ask if they wants to help pick out clothes for the day. "Do you want to pick out the baby's clothes today?"
- If you are changing a diaper you could ask them, "Oh, can you get mama a new diaper?"

06/ SIBLING SUPPORT

Let's look how we can give your older children some focus. Having a new baby in the home is a big transition for everyone. Here are some simple ways to make sure your older children know you're still there for them.

LOVE

A good idea is to find a doll or stuffed animal to present to the older child. This will give them someone to care for when you need to focus on the baby. They can change their diaper and clothe the stuffy.

ONE ON ONE TIME

This is a big transition for everyone, but especially your older child. They've had you to themselves for so long and now they have to share. Try to set aside one on one time every day, even if it's a 10 minute activity.

WORDS

Changing a few words, can make ALL the difference. Don't blame everything on the baby. Instead of, "After I change the baby, I can help" Say, "I'll help you in three minutes." It's a small change but can have a big impact.

MAMA CHECK IN

CHECK IN

Reading this chapter about setting boundaries with friends and family members, how does it make you feel? Are you confident in setting boundaries and asking for what you need?

Mama, do you feel confident to set the boundaries that are right for your family?

_____
_____
_____
_____
_____
_____
_____

What are you worried about when it comes to setting boundaries?

_____
_____
_____
_____
_____
_____
_____

POSTPARTUM PLAN

REFLECTION

What do your boundaries for visitors look like? Will you set visiting hours? Will anyone visit at the hospital? How do you keep your boundaries once the baby arrives?

What boundaries will you have for visitors in early postpartum?

_____
_____
_____
_____
_____
_____
_____

How will you communicate these boundaries?

_____
_____
_____
_____
_____
_____
_____
_____

POSTPARTUM PLAN

REFLECTION

What role with the grandparents play? Remember this is your postpartum plan, they don't get to tell you what's right in terms of visiting or helping. What works for your family?

How will the grandparents support your postpartum experience?

_____
_____
_____
_____
_____
_____
_____

Are there any boundaries you will set? (ex. hospital visits, contacting before coming over, helping)

_____
_____
_____
_____
_____
_____
_____
_____

POSTPARTUM PLAN

BRAINSTORM

What does the transition look like welcoming a baby home? How can you support your older children? Brainstorm some ideas with your partner. The language you can use, how to create one on one time and when to introduce your older child to the baby.

What are some simple ideas for one on one time with your older child?

_____
_____
_____
_____
_____
_____
_____

How can you work together to use supportive language for your older child when it comes to the baby?

_____
_____
_____
_____
_____
_____
_____
_____

"SETTING BOUNDARIES IN POSTPARTUM IS GIVING YOURSELF PERMISSION TO TAKE CARE OF YOU, SO YOU CAN BETTER CARE FOR YOUR LITTLE ONE."

Tijana

Chapter 07

POSTPARTUM PARTNER PLANNING

HOW CAN YOU START THE CONVERSATION BEFORE THE BABY ARRIVES AND MAKE A GREAT PLAN

PARTNER PLAN

Sitting down to create a plan with your partner is crucial for your postpartum support mama. This will start great communication between the two of you. No matter what arises you will have a plan and if you don't you will know how to touch base with one another. Mark and I had a plan for our babies but not for us and this made early postpartum very difficult.

Postpartum is important for mama but also the partner. Their life is also changing in a big way. What does sleep look like for everyone? Will your partner help with feedings? How do you still focus on your relationship and take time for each other? This is a plan you make together. Set aside time for this part of the book so you can read through the partner plan sections and answer the postpartum prompts together.

Making a Plan Together

07 / POSTPARTUM PARTNER PLAN

This part of the postpartum planner is meant to be completed with your partner. Set aside time where you can sit down together an review. This section is less about education and more about reflection. This is part of the postpartum plan where you need to work together so you both feel supported.

RESPONSIBILITES: Who will take care of what, and maybe will it look different than it does now? What does your sleep look like? Who will take care of the household chores? Can you share the feedings?

SLEEP: It's so important in early postpartum. Create a sleep plan for your family. Where will the baby sleep? How will you support each other's sleep?

RELATIONSHIP: The relationship with your partner will be even more crucial in early postpartum. You will support one another but also need to find time to be together. What's are things you enjoy doing together?

SELF-CARE: Perhaps you have time for self-care now without scheduling it. Once the baby arrives it's good for both of you to make sure you are finding time for things that recharge you and are something you enjoy.

MENTAL HEALTH: Checking in with one another to make sure you are feeling yourself in postpartum. Your doctor will ask the questions, but your partner knows you best. Touching base with each other regularly to see how you are doing and also watching for the signs of any PMAD's is essential.

WORK: Every family plan is different. How long will your partner have off? Will you have a maternity leave and what does that look like? Although it's sad to think about it's good to know the plan so you can also discuss budget, childcare and any concerns.

HOUSEHOLD RESPONSIBILITIES

HOW CAN YOU MAKE POSTPARTUM SMOOTH AND SUPPORTIVE

Postpartum is not the time to be fighting over who is going to do the dishes or make dinner. It's a time to support each other, work together and try and make everyone feel good.

HOUSEHOLD DUTIES
List all household duties

MAMA RESPONSIBILITES
List all household duties

PARTNER RESPONSIBILITIES
List all household duties

POSTPARTUM SLEEP

PLAN TO GET THE MOST SLEEP AND WHERE WILL BABY SLEEP?

Having an idea of how you can support each other's sleep will be a very good start to postpartum. Making a plan for where the baby will sleep allows you to be on the same page.

WHERE WILL THE BABY SLEEP?	
DAY	NIGHT

MAMA SLEEP & FEED SCHEDULE	
TIME	ACTIVITY

PARTNER SLEEP & FEED SCHEDULE	
TIME	ACTIVITY

IMPORTANT IN YOUR RELATIONSHIP

YOU AND YOUR PARTNER NEED TO CARVE OUT TIME FOR EACH OTHER

How do you keep the connection between feedings, sleeping and getting through the day? What do you enjoy doing together that you could bring into postpartum? What's important to you and your relationship?

ACTIVITIES YOU LOVE
List what you love to do together

MAMA DATES
What are some simple ways you'd like to connect?

DAD DATES
What activities can you do together at home?

POSTPARTUM SELF-CARE

HOW CAN YOU CARVE OUT TIME FOR SELF-CARE?

What are things that give you energy or make you feel refreshed? Working out? Yoga? A walk? Listening to a podcast? A hot shower/bath? Now how can you make sure you find time for these with a baby?

HOW CAN YOU SUPPORT EACH OTHER
List ways to help create time for self-care

MAMA SELF-CARE
Things that make you feel happy or refreshed

PARTNER SELF-CARE
Ways you can recharge

MENTAL HEALTH

HAVING SOMEONE TO CHECK IN WITH YOU IS IMPORTANT.

Do you and your partner know the difference between the baby blues and postpartum depression? Have you familiarized yourself with the PMAD's? Being able to recognize the signs and ask the right questions can make all the difference.

DO YOU KNOW THE DIFFERENCE?
List the differences between baby blues and PPD

MAMA CHECK IN
Questions you can ask.

PARTNER CHECK IN
Questions to touch base.

BACK TO WORK

DO YOU HAVE A MATERNITY PLAN? HOW LONG WILL YOU HAVE OFF?

Does your partner have some days off after the baby is born? What does that look like? Do you have a maternity leave, how long? Once you're both back to work do you have childcare or support?

MAMA TIME OFF
How long? Back to work date?

PARTNER TIME OFF
How long? Back to work date? Any vacation days?

CHILDCARE BRAINSTORM
Childcare in your area? Applying to waitlists.

"THIS IS A NEW CHAPTER TOGETHER AS PARENTS, WHERE EVERY MOMENT IS A CHANCE TO LEARN, GROW, AND LOVE EACH OTHER EVEN MORE."

Tijana

Chapter 08

YOUR POSTPARTUM SUPPORT TEAM

ALL THE WONDERFUL PEOPLE WHO CAN HELP YOU DURING POSTPARTUM

HELPING HANDS: YOUR SUPPORT TEAM

I believe one of the most important parts of your postpartum plan is your support team. When I had difficulty breastfeeding and a low milk supply, I was sent a local lactation consultant. I never had the chance to interview them or see if our feeding values aligned. They didn't. After the appointment I felt defeated, ashamed and like I'd failed as a mama.

Take a minute to consider your postpartum support. Who is on your team? Are there people that come to mind immediately? Have you already spoken to a few people? Are you not sure where to start? Over the next few pages we will discuss and build your support team. Touching base with this list of people prior to the birth of your baby, whether paid help or family and friends. Outlining how you'd like them to assist you on your postpartum journey and sharing anything from your postpartum plan that would be helpful.

Creating the Dream Team

08 / POSTPARTUM SUPPORT

Building a strong postpartum support team is so important for your well-being and adjustment into motherhood. Let's start to brainstorm who can be on your postpartum support team and we will start planning over the next few weeks.

PARTNER: Your partner plays a vital role in providing emotional support, helping with household tasks, assisting with the baby care and making sure you're getting enough sleep.

FAMILY: Grandparents, aunts, siblings or other close family members can offer help in the home, emotional support, knowledge and give you rest.

FRIENDS: Close friends can be good for emotional support, think of the people who you could call in moments where you need someone to listen. Are there other new mamas in your community you can connect with? Stroller walks can be a lifesaver!

POSTPARTUM DOULAS: These are trained professionals who will help you with physical and emotional support. They can also provide guidance on baby care, breastfeeding, and household tasks.

LACTACTION CONSULTANTS: If you're wanting to breastfeed, lactation consultants can offer expert advice and guidance. They can address any challenges that may be coming up.

MENTAL HEAL PROFESSIONALS: If you don't currently have a therapist or counselor I believe it can be really beneficial in early postpartum to have outside support. They can address any concerns with postpartum depression, help you with the transition into motherhood and more.

PARENTING SUPPORT GROUPS: Research groups in your area. Whether it's a mama's support group or mommy and me class, where are there opportunities to create community.

ONLINE COMMUNITIES: If you're wanting to stay closer to home in early postpartum. Look into supportive online communities where you can seek advice or do a virtual meet up.

SUPPORTING REST

WHO CAN HELP IN THE EARLY DAYS OF POSTPARTUM

Add family, friends as well as paid services that can support you in the early newborn days or after your partner goes back to work.

DURING THE DAY	
NAME	CONTACT

DURING THE NIGHT	
NAME	CONTACT

EARLY EVENINGS	
NAME	CONTACT

SUPPORTING BREASTFEEDING

WHO CAN HELP WITH YOUR BREASTFEEDING JOURNEY

You will need to find your breastfeeding rhythm. During this time it's good to surround yourself with knowledgeable and supportive people.

FRIENDS OR FAMILY WHO SUPPORT YOUR FEEDING CHOICES	
NAME	CONTACT

LACTACTION CONSULTANTS WHO ALIGN WITH YOUR FEEDING CHOICES	
NAME	CONTACT

LOCAL BREASTFEEDING SUPPORT GROUPS BOTH VIRTUAL AND IN PERSON	
NAME	CONTACT

SIBLING SUPPORT

THOSE WHO WILL CARE FOR YOUR OLDER CHILD

It's good to have options for older children when you're in labor and in early postpartum. This can help everyone with this big transition.

WHO WILL BE AVAILABLE TO BE WITH YOUR OLDER CHILD DURING BIRTH?	
NAME	CONTACT

PEOPLE WHO ARE AVAILABLE FOR QUIALITY TIME, PLAYDATES OR HELPING WITH DROP OFF	
NAME	CONTACT

PAID SUPPORT FORWITH DAYCARE DAYS, DROP INS AND HALF DAY PROGRAMS	
NAME	CONTACT

MAMA SUPPORT

HOW CAN YOU CARE AND SUPPORT YOURSELF IN POSTPARTUM

These are options to help you with your household, body and mental health. Taking care of yourself is the most important mama!

WHO CAN HELP SUPPORT YOUR BODIES HEALING AFTER BIRTH? (massage, pelvic floor therapist, osteopath)

NAME	CONTACT

THOSE YOU TRUST TO DISCUSS HOW YOU ARE FEELING AND COPING. (friends, family, counsellor, mama groups)

NAME	CONTACT

SUPPORT IF YOU'RE FEELING OVERWHELMED. (cleaner, friend or family to help with the baby or household)

NAME	CONTACT

"PLANNING ALLOWS US TO CREATE A POSTPARTUM VILLAGE BEFORE THE BABY ARRIVES. NOT HOPING ONE WILL SHOW UP WHEN THE BABY IS BORN."

Tijana

Chapter 09

YOU'VE GOT THIS MAMA!

NOW YOU HAVE THE TOOLS AND INFORMATION TO MAKE SURE YOU FEEL CONFIDENT AND SUPPORTED

YOUR POSTPARTUM PLAN

Mama, you've made it through your postpartum plan. I hope you feel confident, supported and excited for the fourth trimester. This postpartum planner is meant to be used. Leave it out for yourself or your partner to reference. In hard moments or times of doubt, take five minutes to review your plan or the are you're struggling with. This isn't simply a planner, but a tool with important postpartum information.

You are about to embark on an amazing journey into motherhood. No one can prepare you for this. It will be joyful, beautiful, hard but worth it. I hope this postpartum planner I created with love and reflection on my own postpartum journey will allow you to ask for help when you need it, understand that you are learning to be a mama and know you will get this through postpartum phase.

You've Done it Mama!

09 / YOU'VE GOT THIS MAMA!

Look at all the areas you've learned about, taken the time to reflect on what's right for your family and written out a postpartum plan to make sure you feel confident and supported in the postpartum period.

Postpartum nutrition to support your body, healing and energy.

PAGE 29

Becoming a mama, the emotional and physical changes.

PAGE 45

Getting to know your baby, understanding a newborn.

PAGE 67

Family education, boundaries, sibling support, visitors.

PAGE 87

Partner plan creating a plan together and reflecting on what's important.

PAGE 101

Your support team, family, friends, community and paid.

PAGE 113

09 / HOSPITAL BAG CHECKLIST

FOR MOM

- [ ] PURSE
- [ ] INSURANCE CARD & ID
- [ ] DEVICE CHARGERS
- [ ] SNACKS/LARGE WATER BOTTLE
- [ ] LIP BALM
- [ ] BODY LOTION
- [ ] GLASSES/CONTACTS
- [ ] DRY SHAMPOO
- [ ] NIPPLE CREAM
- [ ] TOOTHPASTE/TOOTH BRUSH
- [ ] MOUTHWASH/FLOSS
- [ ] DEODORANT
- [ ] HAIR TIES/HAIRBRUSH
- [ ] MAKEUP
- [ ] NURSING PADS
- [ ] SOCKS
- [ ] SLIPPERS WITH ANTI-SLIP GRIPS
- [ ] STRETCHY CLOTHES
- [ ] IPAD/BOOKS/ENTERTAINMENT
- [ ] GOING-HOME OUTFIT
- [ ] NURSING BRA (SIZE UP!)
- [ ] DARK, FRONT-OPENING SHIRTS

FOR BABY

- [ ] PACIFIERS
- [ ] HAT AND MITTENS
- [ ] SWADDLING BLANKETS
- [ ] BABY NAIL FILE
- [ ] BURP CLOTH
- [ ] CAR SEAT
- [ ] NURSING PILLOW
- [ ] ONESIES
- [ ] SOCKS
- [ ] GOING HOME OUTFIT
- [ ] SLEEPSACKS

IMPORTANT

- [ ] HOSPITAL PAPERWORK
- [ ] OB/PEDIATRICIAN INFO
- [ ] BIRTH PLAN

FOR SUPPORT PERSON

- [ ] SNACKS AND DRINKS
- [ ] ENTERTAINMENT
- [ ] DEVICE CHARGERS
- [ ] PILLOW & BLANKET
- [ ] TOILETRIES
- [ ] CHANGE OF CLOTHES
- [ ] REUSABLE WATER BOTTLE

09 / BIRTH PLAN

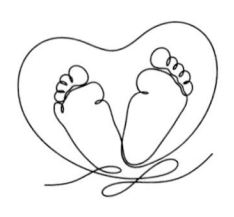

HEALTH INFO

FIRST PREGNANCY?   Y   N

GESTATIONAL DIABESTES?   Y   N

RH INCOMPATABILITY?   Y   N

ALLERGIES?   Y   N

STREP B POSITIVE?   Y   N

HERPES?   Y   N

OTHER: _____

PLANNED BIRTH TYPE:

V-BAC   VAGINAL   C-SECTION

INDUCTION   HOME   WATER

BASIC INFO

FULL NAME:

SUPPORT PERSON'S NAME:

DOCTOR/MIDWIFE:

INSURANCE:

DUE DATE:

DURING LABOR

PAIN MANAGEMENT

- [ ] GOAL IS UNMEDICATED BIRTH
- [ ] ONLY OFFER PAIN MEDS IF ASKED
- [ ] I MAY WANT AN EPIDURAL
- [ ] I MAY WANT IV PAIN MEDS
- [ ] I MAY WANT NITROUS OXIDE
- [ ] BREATHING EXERCISES
- [ ] MASSAGE
- [ ] WALKING/MOVEMENT
- [ ] POSITIVE AFFIRMATIONS
- [ ] HOT/COLD COMPRESS
- [ ] COUNTER PRESSURE
- [ ] SHOWER OR BATH
- [ ] _____
- [ ]

LABOR

- [ ] ACCESS TO BIRTHING COMFORT OPTIONS
- [ ] ABILITY TO LABOR IN ANY POSITION
- [ ] FOOD & DRINK
- [ ] FREEDOM TO MOVE ABOUT

ENVIRONMENT

- [ ] DIM LIGHTING
- [ ] CALMING MUSIC
- [ ] AROMATHERAPY
- [ ] NECESSARY PERSONNEL ONLY
- [ ] LIMITED CERVICAL CHECKS
- [ ] _____

09 / BIRTH PLAN (cont.)

AFTER BIRTH

- ☐ IMMEDIATE SKIN-TO-SKIN
- ☐ DELAYED CORD CLAMPING
- ☐ CORD TO BE CUT BY SUPPORT PERSON
- ☐ CORD TO BE CUT BY STAFF
- ☐ WIPE VERNIX FIRST
- ☐ LEAVE VERNIX ON BABY
- ☐

- ☐ STAFF ANNOUNCE BABY'S SEX
- ☐ SUPPORT PERSON ANNOUNCE BABY'S SEX
- ☐ FIND OUT BABY'S SEX MYSELF
- ☐ SAVE PLACENTA
- ☐ KEEP BABY WITHIN SIGHT OF MOM
- ☐ _____
- ☐

NEWBORN CARE

- ☐ VITAMIN K (ORAL)
- ☐ VITAMIN K (INJECTION)
- ☐ HEP B
- ☐ EYE OINTMENT
- ☐ DELAY BABY'S FIRST BATH
- ☐ _____

- ☐ BREASTFEEDING
- ☐ BOTTLE FEEDING
- ☐ FORMULA
- ☐ NO PACIFIER
- ☐ IF BABY IS MALE: CIRCUMCISE
- ☐ IF BABY IS MALE: DO NOT CIRCUMCISE

ADDITIONAL PREFERENCES/NOTES

09 / PADSICLE INSTRUCTIONS

A padsicle can become your best friend when dealing with postpartum pain. A padsicle is basically a pad that is chilled in the freezer and then after birth placed in your underwear to relieve pain and encourage healing after a vaginal delivery. If you've had a c-section you can place the pad on top of your scar.

STEP 1
Unwrap a sanitary napkin or pad. Lay it on top of a piece of aluminum foil. The back of the pad will stick to the foil. Remove the tabs to open the pad fully

STEP 2
Spread unscented 100% pure aloe vera gel generously over the pad. Apply the gel with the back of the spoon. Aloe vera can help relieve inflammation and acute pain.

STEP 3
Pour or spray alcohol-free witch hazel over the pad. Witch hazel can reduce swelling, pain or bruising. Will help relieve itching and inflammation from hemorrhoids

STEP 4
Optional, add 1 or 2 drops of lavender essential oil onto the pad. Lavender oil has anti-inflammatory properties, and can help with anxiety and stress.

STEP 5
After applying the aloe vera, witch hazel and lavender oil, gently fold the aluminum foil over the pad. Place the wrapped pad in the freezer for at least an hour.

STEP 6
Prepare several padsicles at once so you have a supply. Don't oversaturate the pad as you still want the pad to be able to absorb postpartum bleeding.

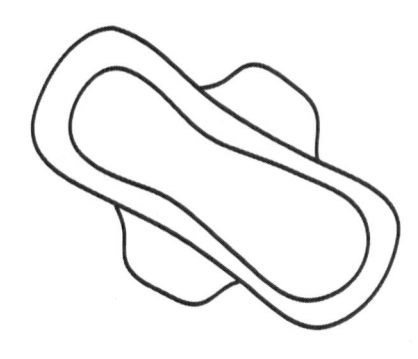

09 / FEEDING & DIAPER CART

Mama, are you ready to have everything you need in one place? The breastfeeding/diaper cart is a great trick to help in postpartum. It keeps everything you need in one place and you can easily move it through the house as needed.

TOP TIER

- [ ] LARGE WATER BOTTLE
- [ ] SELF CARE ITEMS (hair ties, lotion, oils, hand sanitizer)
- [ ] NIPPLE CARE (breast pads, milk supplements, nipple ointment)
- [ ] SNACK BIN (trail mix, granola bars, protein bars)
- [ ] HAIR BRUSH FOR YOU & BABY
- [ ] BABY NAIL SCISSORS
- [ ] BABY SOCKS
- [ ] EXTRA LONG PHONE CHARGER
- [ ] EARBUDS
- [ ] JOURNAL & PEN

SECOND TIER

- [ ] PUMP
- [ ] EXTRA BOTTLES
- [ ] BIN FOR EXTRA BOTTLE LIDS
- [ ] BAG WITH EXTRA PUMP PARTS
- [ ] EXTRA NURSING BRA
- [ ] HAAKA (for nursing)
- [ ] NURSING PILLOW
- [ ] GAS DROPS
- [ ] VITAMIN D DROPS

THIRD TIER

- [ ] DIAPERS & WIPES
- [ ] DIAPER CREAM
- [ ] BURP CLOTHES
- [ ] EXTRA SWADDLES BLANKETS
- [ ] EXTRA ONESIES AND FOOTIES
- [ ] PAJAMAS
- [ ] NOSE ASPIRATOR
- [ ] SOOTHER
- [ ] TOYS OR BOOKS FOR OLDER CHILDREN

09 / BIRTH STORY

Mama, It's so important to reflect on your birth and write down the story of how your baby was born. Use this page to share the details of how your baby was born and all the details of their birth.

FULL NAME			
DATE OF BIRTH		EYE COLOR	
WEIGHT		HAIR COLOR	
LENGTH		TYPE OF BIRTH	
APGAR SCORE		WHO CUT THE CORD	
TIME YOU WERE BORN		WHERE YOU WERE BORN	
WHO CAME TO SEE YOU		DOCTOR/ MIDWIFE	

MY LABOR STORY

09 / LETTER TO YOUR POSTPARTUM BODY

Having a baby and becoming a mama is a life changing experience. Everything changes in an instant and so does your body. It can be a difficult transition. Your wardrobe no longer fits, you may feel uncomfortable in your body and be unhappy with what you see in the mirror. Take the time to write a letter to your postpartum body and all the reasons you love it.

DEAR POSTPARTUM BODY,

"

"MAMA YOU'VE DONE SOMETHING EXTRAORDINARY, SUPPORTING YOURSELF BEFORE THE BABY ARRIVES."

Tijana

Chapter 10

THANK YOU!

I APPRECIATE YOUR TRUST ON THIS JOURNEY TO CREATING A POSTPARTUM PLAN

THANK YOU MAMA

Mama, thank you for trusting me to help you create a postpartum plan. After becoming a mama to twins in 2020 thinking I was TOTALLY prepared. I soon realized I hadn't prepared for the most important part of the postpartum period, ME! Since then I've made it my mission to help mamas feel prepared BEFORE the baby arrives. Creating a plan for themselves, their baby and family.

As you welcome your baby you will be armed with information on healing, a support team, a wonderful partner plan and an understanding of a newborn. Becoming a mama is lifechanging. Remember to focus on the moments of joy and not let the hard or overwhelming moments take the focus.

Enjoy your Fourth Trimester!

POSTPARTUM DOULA

I became a postpartum doula on naptime when our twins were one years old. During my postpartum period I continually had to advocate for myself, ask questions and search for answers in the middle of the night. As a postpartum doula I support mamas in person and virtually as well as host workshops to help them feel confident and supported. If you need further assistance or have questions, I am always available to help.
hello@flourishingpostpartum.com

Mama, I hope this postpartum planner has relieved some of your stress, anxiety and worry. If you have more questions speak with your partner, family, OBGYN, lactation consultant, to get the answers you need.

Tijana

"

I AM THE RIGHT MAMA FOR MY BABY. WITH LOVE AS MY GUIDE AND STRENGTH IN MY EMBRACE, I NAVIGATE THIS BEAUTIFUL JOURNEY OF MOTHERHOOD WITH CONFIDENCE AND GRACE.

Mama Affirmation

Manufactured by Amazon.ca
Acheson, AB